# PATIENCE WITH EACH ROTATION OF THE EARTH

# *Patience With Each Rotation of the Earth*

A collection of poems
by
**DONNY BARILLA**

Adelaide Books
New York / Lisbon
2020

PATIENCE WITH EACH ROTATION OF THE EARTH
A collection of poems
By Donny Barilla

Copyright © by Donny Barilla
Cover design © 2020 Adelaide Books

Published by Adelaide Books, New York / Lisbon
adelaidebooks.org

Editor-in-Chief
Stevan V. Nikolic

All rights reserved. No part of this book may be reproduced in any manner whatsoever without written permission from the author except in the case of brief quotations embodied in critical articles and reviews.

For any information, please address Adelaide Books
at info@adelaidebooks.org
or write to:
Adelaide Books
244 Fifth Ave. Suite D27
New York, NY, 10001

ISBN: 978-1-951896-34-8

Printed in the United States of America

*To Lisa the Potter*

# *Contents*

Past the Fabric of the Field  *17*

Speaking  *18*

Chapel  *19*

Autumn Screams  *20*

Hour of Scarlet  *21*

After the Rain  *22*

Lost by Nightfall  *23*

Morning Walk  *24*

Reading the Manuscript  *25*

I Found Her in the Valley  *26*

Change of Current  *27*

Forever Searching  *28*

Grooming Wheat  *29*

*Donny Barilla*

Questing in the Forest  *30*

Sundance  *31*

Hymnals  *32*

Spring Recollection  *33*

Frozen Ribs  *34*

When the Mourning Dove Calls  *35*

Orchid with the Smash of the Sun  *36*

Snowy Meadow  *37*

As the Gardener Works Alone  *38*

Quest Leads to the Bones of the Woodlands  *39*

Weeping for Porridges  *40*

Scenes of the Passing Crows  *41*

Wading Through the Sweat of Summer  *45*

Autumn Blend  *46*

Covenant  *47*

Coffee Before Dawn  *48*

Scented Creams  *49*

Return to Spring  *50*

Mountain Dust  *51*

*PATIENCE WITH EACH ROTATION OF THE EARTH*

Freshness Beneath the Glaze  **52**

Beyond the Storm I Starve Past Thicket and Thorn  **53**

From Bog to Mountain Rise  **54**

Found Spirits  **55**

Return  **56**

Reds and Navies  **57**

Patience  **58**

Blossoming Buds and Crackling Branches  **59**

Moments of Summer  **60**

Rest in the Forest Until the End of Hours  **61**

Heading West  **63**

From the Cabin to Fellowship in the Woods  **64**

Charms of the River Passing  **65**

Fields of Wheat  **66**

Flesh of the Moon  **67**

Wooded Echo  **68**

Orchid Bellows to the Rising Myth  **69**

Clovers at the Depth of Night  **70**

Milking Acorns  **71**

Shift as Twilight Comes   *75*

Tender Bones   *76*

Wicker Chair   *77*

By Nightfall   *78*

Evening Scene   *79*

Beneath the Linen Sheets   *80*

Caught in the Summer Blaze   *81*

Fields Glazed   *82*

Stumble on the Mountainside   *83*

Phantom in the Late Hour of Autumn   *84*

Fist of Leaves   *85*

Resting on the Field of Jade   *86*

Resurrection   *87*

Blackbird Return   *88*

Blouse Loosens   *89*

Long Shadows of December   *90*

Passing Seasons   *91*

Awakening to Stillness   *92*

Lavender Blouse   *93*

PATIENCE WITH EACH ROTATION OF THE EARTH

Carving Fingers  *94*

Puzzles  *97*

Loss  *98*

Waiting With the Willow Tree  *99*

Particles of Preservation  *100*

Awoken I Cast the Longest Shadow  *101*

In the Attic Room  *102*

Leaves Hung of the Frozen Floor  *103*

Spread of Apricot  *104*

Earliest Moment  *105*

Golds  *106*

Ribs of Autumn  *107*

Searching for the Coast  *108*

Opened as Goblets  *109*

Seeds Upon the Wind  *110*

Return to the Fields in the Mourning Hour  *111*

Waiting  *112*

Back to the Forest  *113*

By the Cove  *114*

Donny Barilla

Coated in Gold  *115*

Fade of Her Shadow  *116*

Bluebird  *117*

Ocean Walk in the Deep of Night  *118*

Blood Upon the Grass of Jade  *119*

White Petal  *120*

Remembrances by the Garden  *121*

Passages  *125*

Hollow of the Pocket  *126*

Entering the Passage of Winter  *127*

Dipped in the Wilt of Autumn  *128*

Upon the Mountaintop  *129*

Quilt  *130*

Winter Shoal  *131*

Rains in the Bay  *132*

Rain Storm  *133*

Thin Stem  *134*

Chipped and Wooden  *135*

By the Pond  *136*

Vest and Fiber  *137*

Mercy  *138*

Chasing the Endless Court  *139*

Creek  *140*

Garment and Jacket  *141*

Fleece  *142*

In the Garden  *143*

Egret  *144*

As He Waits for Spring  *145*

About the Author  *149*

*I mourn this loss of the gown of Autumn.*

*By early day, I welcome the spirited rain.*

Past the Fabric of the Field

I sat upon the porch overlooking the spread
which stretched across the tangled grass and weeds
of the lusty, fertile earth.

The breathing air swept and enticed the dew
as every spot of clover and shoot shook loose
the beads as they soaked into the caked clays and patch
of gentle mud.

Drinking the steamy treasure of this blistering coffee,
I soothed the parched wilt of my throat.

By midday, I walked through to the end of the grotto.
I fished the channel and rapids of the slicing stream.

With warmth, the descending air tangled and pressed
as each small wave of the creek, giggled with rapture
as the dancing threads slipped away,
fumbling cotton moisture.

I turned and walked through the meadow.
From a far distance, I caught sight of my home
which stood as a sentinel awaiting my return.

Speaking

I spoke to the lavish gray speckled sky.

Winds coarsed through the full bloom of my hair
which relished in soothing delight
of each strand of this chestnut hue.

I reached my fingers in approval as the dense
gathering of warm Summer's breath sharpened
across my yearning face.

Walking further, I stepped through into the meadows
as they stretched for miles and neighbored threads of grass
boasting of their lusty roots.

Upon the sting of my sight,
the turning winds slapped and swarmed across my face.

By nightfall, I walked swift and bloomed
my touch to the tender earth.

Chapel

I pinched the slithering aroma as it
trellised throughout the room.
Empty. The chapel sang to the wrapping winds
shooting across the brim of the angled roof. Standing still, I
listened to the patterns of an ancient alphabet
which tugged my flesh, bones
in the swift rattle of the glass and chipped wooden pews.

Softly, I tasted the bloods of the vine as the drift of each
smothering jaunt, vanilla and sandalwood,
took me to the breast
of her which soothed and silenced me.

The smother of my words fell upon me.
I mulled the eclipse of the dome.
Walking home, the weeds rose through crack and edge.
I paused and looked to the spread of the meadow
and walked to the prism of approaching night.

Autumn Screams

I ask of the wind to shroud me in petals and wash me
with fragrances of the sour mumbling mulch.

I leaned gently to the floods of dancing breath.
Every grassy spear hooks across my ankle and foot.

Crunch of the pinecone shouted aloud in desperate regret
as the needled bed softened the moaning
chip and wooden piece.

Looking about this forest, I hear the screams of Autumn.
I walk to the treasures and charms of
this deeply shadowed nightfall.

I dripped in the pause of white dewdrops.
Tasting the blood of the earth, this
dampness relishes within me.

Watching the slant of the sun, I gripped upon my skin
the longest shadows and the spread of the leafy fleece
which rolls and tamps upon the crusted floor.

Hour of Scarlet

The hyacinth bled violets with quivers
of each soft petal and flickering
dance of the midday sun.

Leaning to the pouch of pollens in the face of the flower,
I breathe the life of the meadow and spreading field.

With a quake across the thin stretch of the pampering clouds,
the hot breath of this Summer storm cracked in the deep
edge of the most distant field.

Standing, I courted the jade grasses and
stiffness of the onion sprout.
The sky became electric blue
as I walked swiftly to the haunch of my home.

I awoke in the tangled arms of soft blankets and a tender
dash of snapping embers of the ancient brick fireplace.

I listened to the peppering crimp of the raindrops.
Leaning into the lift of the threads of each pillow, I
mumbled to the smacking wood of the roof.

I awoke in this hour of heavy scarlet
which soothed the depress
of my swimming head and neck.

After the Rain

Silent soil beneath the softest spread of the moss
which rested the bones of my head and neck,
I lay in eternal sleep as the gentle wind crossed me
and tossed tufts of my hair, so waved and full.

Upon opening my eyes, I stood to a slouch as the wilt
of these whicker bones and I stood witness
to the surfacing rain which moistened
each fabric and strand of hair as I walked to the porch,
well snug under the trees, dancing eaves.

I roamed the avenue to the warmth of my bed
which tapered the quietest linens, wrapping across
the nakedness of my old body.

I slept again until the ivories of the sky
swept and sank to the paleness of my withered skin.

I awoke through the flesh of the earth.

Lost by Nightfall

At twelve thirty her flesh soaked into the soil
and soothed her to the voices of each stretch of dirt
and capsules of a heavy clay.

Flowers suckled into the earth and cast fragrance
upon the looseness of her ancient breasts;
walking home I felt the voices of the closeness
of the creek.

Looking upon a curving rapid, I watched the friendship
of a yellow rose fumble it's way across the soft rocks.

I gathered myself and continued upon
the swerves and cuts of the creek.
Well into nightfall, I lost my way and grew in the covenant
of the wild grip of forest and sudden grotto.

Morning Walk

I sang tenderly to the scuffling brown tree leaves of Autumn
as chilled fingers and palms soothed
across the sting of my face.

Broomed in winds which wrap across
the width of my chest, I
speak of the lusty tremble of weeds and long lasting ferns.

The groan of my voice travels through
the narrowest stretch of woods.
I listen to my echo as it scours across
the meadow, filling her ears.

There soaks a passage of fragrant wind
which fills my lungs with dusts, vibrant
soaking edge of each pine.

I return at the gentle quake of morning
peach and violet hues.

The sweet lush of the moist earth coddles me in moans
shouting out from the splashes of early sunlight.

Reading the Manuscript

Breath exhumed the openness of her mouth,
leaving vacancy with the tremble of her tongue,
preserving the endless humidity as I filled the spaces
around her soft warmth.

I paused as her hands swept beneath the cottons of my shirt.
Here, I discovered the majesty of the
yellow dash of the rising sun.

I drank from her with the soaked edges of the moonlit hours.

Again, I returned to the buttered landscape of morning.
I sculpted the manuscript of a teasing wind.

I Found Her in the Valley

Water trickled across the mountains
boulders and slippery rocks.
Listening to her heaving lungs, I mourned with her
as the clouds fell and I washed my face with her ash gray hair.

Turning to her, I broadened my hands and placed them upon
my thudding temples.

The slapping winds stood beyond me and rambled
across the flesh as I surrendered to the
silence of the mountainside.

I found passage to the glen, saddled low
in the valley and sipped the rose
water from the cup of the blooming bud.

I stopped and rested in this lusty
garden, filled with the maple,
the climbing pine.

This tender valley sloped as her fertile
thighs, quivered in anticipation.

I groomed my way through maize and fields of wheat.
Sweetly, I felt the burn of the sun, tangled
through clouds and ancient vapors.

Change of Current

The pond layered in cakes of ice, trembling
maple leaves scurried across leaving a whispering current.

I threw slender stones across the sleek press
of this Wintery slab.

Moments later, the blitz of the sun angled through
gray pasture of the sky.

I shown my face upon the yellow creams of the sun.
My face loosened and took to the parted beams.

I turned and faced the scattered and broken trail.
Dusts of white took to the sweeping winds, I

walked upon the dancing mountain's edge of my feet,
the forest gathered me in the grace of
it's pines and tender cones.

Forever Searching

The rain stung with the piercing gallop of heavens
fresh distribution.

I fondled the puddles, murky and shallow by the roadside
as throttling cars dashed by carving
their way to the distant routes
headed for the climbing peak of moaning mountainside.

Upon pausing and looking to the sobbing fields of maize,
I pressed foot by foot and sank into the heaviest of muds.

Leagues of acres passed and I reach the
crowned edge of the woods.

Each soft aroma of this ripe conservation
tossed pollens and seeds
across the curves of my face as the popping
pods swelled in my parted mouth.

I knelt to the patch of mushrooms and
favored one after another.
Silently I remain poised in the pocket of gushing springs.

Grooming Wheat

Her flesh brought life into the pouch of my mouth.

I step so slight into the flicker of each
stalk of grooming wheat.
Sun dancing, I felt it's grip upon the back of my neck.

~

I entered this wealth of the rambling kitchen.
I smelled the dough as it rose, then fell.

Powdery flour smacked against the crest of your apron
which pronounced every lush and phonic.

Upon losing my way beneath you,
I felt the stride of your thighs which soaked white pearl beads
and bloomed your slick
hair which stuck in fevers to your thudding temples.

~

The fields chilled with the approach of quivering night.
Her scent clung to me as boots to most fertile mud and clay.

I slept in the sauces of night and woke
to the fevers of morning light,
cascading upon us.

Questing in the Forest

I found you well into the deep.
Thick vines climbed and wrapped with all the rise and fall
which released to the snap of the axe.

I fumbled upon you as leaves fluttering across the soil
and hard clays of the forests earth.

Perched rain gathered in the hollow of the tender oak tree.
Secretly, I drank and blossomed to the grazing winds.

As I sat upon the fallen tree log, there I found you.
You crawled across the flesh of my arms and legs.

Dusts took to the sweet wind as I smiled
and tasted the moments
dancing in currents; I recall the flesh of each breasts you
held, so filled with milks.

Sundance

With a snap of the fallen branches and mourn of the twigs
tossed across the woodland floor, I
stepped to the towering reign of the tulip tree.

Moans of the spreading bud,
opening of the virginal petals which tossed their
patient scents to the groan of the fertile earth,

I walked my way across the slender spread
of this place which lives in togetherness.

Each molecule of the trembling forest spoke,
sweet lusts and pulses which soak upon me as well
as each scream and fiber of wooden chip, tossed needles
proud of the pinetree.

I slept for years as the buds grew across me.
I opened myself to the light which flickered
through each wavering leaf.

Softly, I lived for the shift of the sun.

Hymnals

Skipping stones across the film of the pond and there slipped
reflections of the universe in this gentle pasture.

I gathered myself and swept, walked into the heavy wood.

Here, the clutter of the sky, soaking navies which
dance and twirl upon the gusty breeze, fell upon the madness
of the ancient oak and sycamore.

I sat and listened to every bone groomed in the earth.

With pleasantries, I released my ivory breath and this heavy
Autumn sang to me in the scream of a hymnal.

Every branch rattled and served as a choir.

Spring Recollection

From the warm breath of the sky,
tapping the bedroom window,
I angeled my lips upon the openness of her lips.

Folding across her, the down of the pillows sculpted
across the sweats of her head and neck.

I listened to curves of her nakedness and watched each
curl of each finger as they sank into the paleness of my flesh.

Upon the height of the screaming storm,
I crooned and quivered with each
mumbling rattle of the roof.

I returned to her in Spring several years past.

Recalling every movement and pause,
the dome of the heavens
swelled into a gray marble tapestry.

Swiftly, stopping by the rosebuds, acres of
moisture wept at foot and ankle.

Frozen Ribs

White veils slung across the field,
so close to the threads of the icy creek.

My breath bloomed in vapors as they rose
to the brim of the lowest hanging fog.

Feeling the flakes pat upon the edges of my cheeks,
this burning cold stung across me as the fall
of the needled pine tree, soft upon the clay of the earth.

Walking upon the ribs of the frozen soil, I
tamped my way through the death of the grotto
and secretively, I spoke to the powders
which sulk into the deep of the fleece covered ground.

Into the wealth of March, I watched the fog
quietly lift.

Muds returned and I felt the motioned glimmer
upon the wind.

This tease of budding life swelled into the mask of the air.

When the Mourning Dove Calls

I awoke and smelled the scent, fragrance of the infancy
of the budding soil.

Quietly, I spooled the edge of my boots along the wiry
grasses and heard the muffled coo of the mourning dove
freshen across me.

As I turned and faced the breathing press of the eastern
skyline, I embraced the lusty winds as each
fumbling seed danced by grotto and filled the starvation
of each purring garden.

By night, I dreamed of the rooted oak and she wrapped
her branches in strength and quivering buds spoke of her
aptitude and regal prowess.

Orchid with the Smash of the Sun

The orchid pried open beneath the
press of the pale rising sun.

I held the cup of my hands to gather the full blossom
of each dash of clear beads of rain.

With drafty rhythms, the lush flickering petals quivered
soothingly beneath the paints of the remaining moonlight.

After looking upon the flower majestic, sweet flavors
tossed swift into the dance of daylight.

Heel and toe, I penetrated the soils which
carve their way beneath me.

After I pause for a gentle moment,
I watch the white petals curl to the
rise of each smash of the sun.

Snowy Meadow

I fractured the mold with the chisel of my steps.
My boots deepened with each snap, ices and snow drifts
tumbling fine powders across the slithering path of the field.

Listening to the howling sky,
each crackling vowel sauntered through a spindling gasp.

Silently, I stepped across this haze of soft wind.

I returned to the quest in this eggshell, creamy meadow;
clouds lowered and I welcomed each passing breath
as crackling, wintery gauze fattened across my neck and face.

I spoke to the pop of the tree branch.
Every twig suckled into the heavy press where I stretch
quietly and rest beneath the wide spread maple tree

which nurtured me in shelter and a quiet lounge
where the Spring speaks swift into the grooming
tangle of frost and snow.

As the Gardener Works Alone

Ivy webbed between my toes.
Soft, black soil bedded through the steps of these
stiff, calloused feet.

With a swift turn to the spreading gray clouds
stroking across the edges of the forested hills
and the crouch of the haunched cabin, I heard the moans
of the swabbed sun as it launched across the fibers
of the marbled dome.

Earth, from the darkest greens to the trembling
mockery of the scattered clover,
soothed the stride and inch of my ankles and calves.

Well into the deep of twilight,
the sky opened and mulled rains, heavy with craft,
soaked in a mist.

I heard the fangs of the rooted tree, cry aloud, "Rest with me.

I am the trellise of the slumber you crave, desire."

With the fracture of the next morning,
I relish in the sleep of this meadow and spread
of the heaviest greens blooming upon the distant hills.

Quest Leads to the Bones of the Woodlands

I pressed these lips to hers and fell to the quilts
in the warmth of sweet aromas of gravity
which tangle our pulp and flesh well
into the dance of evening.

As I awoke to the rattle of this mad Autumn day,
the flavors of morning pulsed through me in jades
and emeralds of the spreading meadow.

Sleeping into the lancing blades of the moon,
still reaching for the dampness of the horizon,
tenderly, I opened the crest of my eyes.

Soon, I dressed in the quake of the nearby woodlands.

I gathered my things and walked well into the thick
bones of the earth and walked into the fading arrows,
trembling night.

Weeping for Porridges

Drinking the chilled spread of the spiny creek,
I filled my cupped mouth and swooned as the puckering
mouth of an infant.

Every rivet combing the rocky rapids
swept across my tongue as the fullness of a breast
so alive in the foamed milks which
softened as porridges and pulps.

Looking to the smooth lemony cream of the late
Autumn sun, I quivered and stood, only to find
swift steps of my feet tamping the brown soil
of the leathery countryside.

Upon the arrival at the haunched stance
of my home, I slipped through the rickety gait.

I wept across her and touched the majesty
of each full, warm breast.

Scenes of the Passing Crows

Threads of her full, black, silk hair
opened as a roaming murder of crows, so
endless across the tender blue of the sweeping sky.

Welcoming her touch with the glaze of each
iced finger, we groomed into the breath of Winter.

Opened blouse which slipped across the smoothest
of wooden floors, their tangled a choir of the winds
trembling at the french doors; the wicker chairs
screamed across the narrow ledge of the porch.

Snows flooded in veils across the tender grotto.
I whispered in her moist trembling mouth
and soaked upon the warm grip of her Wintery vapors.

*By the middle of day, I witness the cream of the sun rise above the highest summit. I witness the quivering leaves.*

Wading Through the Sweat of Summer

Wading in rhythms high stretched to the waist
as I tremble from the chill and gushing bloods
of the swift creek,
I hear the crickets moan at the deepest hour of day.

The sun soaks beyond the crest of the sparse quivering
forest and I swim my way through the coarse
gritty winds which toss thick, humid warmth.

Searching beneath the ebony sky, I
find the damp scarlet moss and sweetly slumber upon it.

When I awake, the dancing hour of night
soothes my weariness in the heaviest of gripping sweats
which edge there way to this soaked flesh, I walk
the deepest grip, this fumbling sweat of nightfall.

Autumn Blend

With the nimble snap of my fingers and thumb,
I sever the stitch of your blouse and watch
the rise of the peach and indigo sky.

Upon pressing my face to the warmth of your breasts,
filled with milks and pale the color of creams,
I hear the 'coo' of the mourning dove and
soothe to the moaning marrow of the soil beneath me.

Stroke of the warm abdomen, I watch, hear
the rise of the sap, dripping in the speech
of the pinetree which loosens through the countless
trees, open in spices and fragrant aromas.

I fall to the edge where the forest meets the girth
of the fertile meadow.

I touch you upon your thigh as the soak of the dewbead
washes the sting of my feet. As the wash of nightfall
scours the earth, I twitch in this coaxing blend of Autumn.

Covenant

Crystal blue light fractured the dome of the sky.
I listened to the river tapped, unravelling as parchment.

Well into the soft grays which loaf as a quilt, I
soak into the brood of this late Summer gala

where roots and choke of the brown onion stalks
stab to the surrendering storm, headed north.

I remove the paste of this cotton shirt and drift
into the mumble of sleek moisture pressing upon me.

I open my mouth and in a instant, I swallow the flavors
of the neighboring mountains which
slices deeply in my throat.

By morning, I walked the endless borough of tapping
fingers which wake me and greet me with pausing lusts.

Finding this sacrament, I rest in the
muds where I once clamored
with wind, water, and softness of the cupping clover.

Sweetly, I offer my bones to the altar of the earth.

Coffee Before Dawn

Watching the candle toss the thinnest beads
upon the hardwood floor, I cast my gaze through the window
and listened to the groan of the locust.

Mumbling sounds drifted across the lowering thickness
of the gauze spreading through the meadow
which spoke openly before me.

So near the nightstand, I lifted the steam of the mug
and swallowed the hot quiver of coffee
as I waited for morning.

Scented Creams

I walk through the softness, moisture of this full earth.

I moan and mourn with the shattered bones of my ancestors
as each fumbling loose leaf scatters across the mulch,
a mineral rich fragrance, so cool and soothing in grip.

I hear the laughter of these cracking branches.
Looking skyward, the gray marble clouds descend
and pause upon the tip of every tree.

I feed my father and his father the marrow of my bones.

Gentle tickling of the Autumn leaf scatters across me.

This shroud warms me in the heaviest
of earthly scented creams
as the winds and the rains slap upon the soft
blend of this quivering earth.

Return to Spring

I stopped and rested beneath the full
bloomed arms of the oak.

Wind swept across my face and I listened as the creaking
wood charmed my way in a tender moan from breeze
to the dance of eager dominion.

Quiet, silent, I stay here quivering until the lusty
scents and spices of Spring pass me in all my rigidness.

Alone in this open pasture, I moved with each moan
of the unveiling arms of April.

I enter the sauces of greedy, flickering birth.
Softly, the breasts of this jade colored, spreading hill,
I yearn as the flutter of this twig.

I lance my way through the spears of this timeless
grass and joust upon the fevers of the pale, white dew beads
which soften the earth where I rest.

## Mountain Dust

Steep, the mountain path stretched to the thinning
air, a swift deepening of this trembling breath.

Silently, the ices dipped their fangs well into the snowy
press upon the rocks and gloat of the heaviest boulder.

I sat for a moment, then sliced my path through the gouge
of the madness where winds slap the face of each cliff.

Fallen to dust, I fell upon the stone and edge of each pine.

Across the mountain peak, I swiftly gathered to every
valley and patch of desperate grasses.

I bring the raspy voice of each hiker,
farmer and dusts upon the forest pond.

Freshness Beneath the Glaze

You cast glances, glaze upon the fullness of your
doughy breasts.

With trellising choirs of each slither of your voice,
I cast both blouse and garment to the splinters,
the ancient floor.

Thick bloods of the beat of my heart
fastens a tremble upon my mouth and tongue.

These thighs and hamstrings soak in the moisture of every
finger, palm, and thumb.

Into the latest chyme and hour of night, I sleep
to the rise of each breath which softens my cheek,
quiet bones murmur of the freshest blood which courses
through the pale flesh of my veins.

Beyond the Storm I Starve Past Thicket and Thorn

Upon the madness through the sauces
of this forest after rainfall,
screams of the crow penetrates through moisture
and echo across every tree and pastures of mud which soothes
the thornbush and calms the thicket which surrounds.

My gaze fastens upon the muffled groan of the treetop.

Sweet air descends and muscles into the wealth of motion;
drizzling leaves and broken buds, slices of the tree bark
opened to the crimp of a showered mesh.

Facing the north shroud of the tallest mountains,
trembling with evergreens on haunch and gleem.

Tread and slip of the boot, I wander through the green moat,
grass covered at the basin of the path which leads to spiny
paths and stroke the avenue of this crest.

Each mount starved in the thick of Summer.
Muscles of the flesh ache upon this trembling gush of wind.

From Bog to Mountain Rise

Dripped and deepening into the sponge
of the bedded forest floor,
I sank and felt the surrender of the earth give to me
each tossed leaf and thick fluids which pulse to my waist.

Death of the red maple sang to me of charms
which hide cleverly in this gambit of trees and sprawl
of the woodland guise.

With damp skies and a swift humid breeze, I
blistered to the hot press as this madness of Summer
crawled upon me and blinded me with shaved chips of dust,
floundering through the weave of this tangled breath.

After the hours passed, I looked to the sky,
sulking in heavy blues and fresh glint's of the apricot
slant which breached the evening's soft dome,
I left the sting and slashes as the recess of the sun

softly faded passed.

The valley left me with a tangled and trembling loss.

I hike the mountains until they mourn and sulk
to the hills which have been arranged
by feet and slapping winds.

Found Spirits

Vowels suckling across the breathing press of a higher thinned
motion of spread and sweeping bloom where clouds sink and
tremble in the slithering fog, I pause and fill my lungs.

Stopped and silent, I rest by the joust of the evergreens.

Upon opening my eyes, I witness the gauze and cottons
which once flickered from roof of the
pines and their slouching cones.

Cool winds trembles across the edge of my lips.

This log I rest on sends tales and dampens the threads
of patterns which lift me in soaked verbs, so alive

in a harsh murmur of consonants. Softly, I groan in fevers
as the keen glances of my eyes spot a spirited creek.

Return

From fevers dripping across the crack of the windowpane,
I listened to the whistle of the broomed gushing winds.

Smudged tears of the lush Autumn storm, I
soothed my eyes as the rolling tumble of leaves

spoke of their approaching death which
groaned upon the breath
of the heavy sky.

My marrow bled and tangled the soils in fury
with ages to slowly arrive, I am the
tears which tremble and soak
upon the nakedness of your feet.

I feel you press against me as I mourn the loss of bone,
cavity and swell of the lips where once we gathered.

Reds and Navies

Edging into the frail softness of your nape and neck,
sweet fragrances bloom upon my face. I wilt to the sounds
of the rising sun, reds and navies.

I unravel as the groin of the earth, springs and slicing creeks.

Taking a fistful of crackling leaves, each
soars upon the wind and weaves about the mask,
the forest where we lay.

With the soreness of my feet, I take stride into gnarled roots.

I touch the stitches of your blouse; gently
I fall through you as the moisture of my touch coddles
the taste of your soothing flesh.

Patience

Sweat poised upon the powders of your breasts.

I traced my fingers through the silks as soothing
fragrances swam through the stillness of night,
alive in grotto and sweeping in tender winds.

The soils and grass of the earth gathered saps
which clung to the fumbling, crisp leaves, softly dancing.

After pressing my lips upon you, the
rise of the trembling winds
threshed and tossed each fiber of hair.

~

I awoke in the crimp and patient design of morning.

The ancient creek sloshed across the bareness of my flesh
as every groom of the soft silt and slippery rock
placed me upon the ribbed bones of
this slicing gush where waters
greet the slowly descending sky.

Blossoming Buds and Crackling Branches

I went to her in vacancies of the goblet of my mouth
and open jaw.

Alive, I soak in the steams rising from the pastures
of her flesh.

Sweet mulch and aromas of the wild blooming buds,
the scarlet mosses drip beneath the towering trees
which motion me in eager sap.

I drink the humid air and seek every groan
as the crackle of the loose branches
quiver my name in gestures.

As fangs, I sink my feet and hooking toes
swift into the sulking bloom of mint which covet
and drip well into the dew of my eyes and
cast a sting.

I fasten myself to the breast of this doughy blossomed earth.
By nightfall, I loosen myself to the dusts which scatter
both gales and sauce of the jade colored ground.

Moments of Summer

I stroke my foot across the soothing trellise of this kelp;
dripping in waves of green, the pond hosts as a tapestry,
calm I sink so alive.

The earliest moment of Summer, I sink these fingers
deeply into the moist moaning sinch of
bloom and relishing pouches
which root from grasses to whimpering branch.

I open myself as a cave and drink.

I hear the giggling tree top thresh each
twig and each scattering leaf.

I listen to the dome of the quivering dash of warm breath;
tenderly, the sweat of the meadows and
perch of the white dewdrops
which rest upon the veined and cupping leaf, I shift my way
to a seasonal gash, pulsing through me.

The lust of Summer lances in wide margin and waves.

Rest in the Forest Until the End of Hours

I tackled the gush of the winds, sweet
waves of the spoken ebbing wash
of the softest meadow.

Rains saddled my face as needles tossed
in this ruby and gray sky.

Well into this smash of daybreak, I soaked my palms.

Sweetly the cooling and trembling sun
dazzled upon my burdened flesh
which burrowed sweat beneath the
denim and cottons I wore.

Spreading branches of the gathering pines
motioned a cove to the needled
bed where cones whispered of this absence of Winter
and all the moaning wooden chips which
sleep as a soft bed of tender mulch.

The field spread and slithered into the
farthest swoon of washed wet, muds
and my sight trimmed and halted short
of the edge where the forest fell
distant and quivered humbly.

Well into the next glancing threads of

*Donny Barilla*

sun, I walked my way through
the drying beds of the fertile earth.

In a dash, the forest welcomed me with richness and the swift
dampness of the pouring creek.

Quietly I fell soft upon the leaves
which dripped into this trail,
Ferns dance with the wild flowers until nightfall surmounts.

Heading West

As I opened my eyes to the rhythms of
the swelled pounding moon,
silver bloom and fastening winds straddled my lungs,
flickering across the chill of my neck and chest.

I lay in the emptiest of fields and watched as the flushing
sky cast sweet glances upon me.

Tears pulsed from the edge of my pierced stinging eyes.

I remembered how she would rest next to me
with her heaving chest and cast powders of her full, doughy
breasts which swooned my face and aching jaw.

You sauced upon me as the naked sky.

I felt the press of the thin, silk hair which stuck against
the paste and sweat of my temples.

Well into the grasp of morning, I headed west and scurried
against the rising sun. How tenderly I chased the moon.

From the Cabin to Fellowship in the Woods

Every splinter and nook of the ancient home, I
tossed my eyes to the dusts which once kept each
child, man and wife in the covenant of the bloom
rising through the windows and light of the sun,
spackling paleness upon the floor and wooden walls.

The antiquated haunch spoke of tenderness.

As this walk deepened into the woods,
I watched the cedar trees
moan of their lost siblings and the heavy oak
burrowed farthest into the earth and
mourned the branches which
screamed of sorrow and loss.

In equal scents which tossed their way into the lungs
of my ancestors, I breathed the same fumbling aromas
and dipped through this sulking breath of marrow.

The earth shared with clays and heavy mud.
Dusts settled here as I tamped swiftly with my boots.

Charms of the River Passing

The sky snapped and spoke of defeat and all realms
surrounding the slender treasure of a mournful
disposition.

Soaked and sweaty wind bloomed in surface
as the dampness of my boot, motioned forward.

The grayish, black sky swept passed and cleared,
humbly.

Wools and cottons remained soaked as I stopped by the river,
fashioned with endless trees.

I drank in fullness and charms of the clearest water.

Fields of Wheat

Softly, I stepped through the weave of the wheat fields.

For a moment, I stood still and listened to the breathing
sky whip across and tempted the groin of the patterned
earth speak.

The grains dampened along the wedge of my shoes.
Winds lashed across the meandering tassle.

In a fragment of a motioning moment, the field opened,
groomed as the dew and minerals of these soft thighs
cooled, then burned in a blushing fever.

~

I slept in the depressions of the bed.
With window cracked and opened ajar, I
gathered the heaviest of scents and furthered my way
in tease and moans of the wind.

Flesh of the Moon

There spread veins beneath the earth which
bled the dew and slither the falling rain.

Moisture welcomed me in smooth depresses,
an opening to the moans of each rib and fragile bone.

I lean against the red maple as every branch crackled
against every branch.

Well into the sweetest flavors of heavy night, I
stepped my way along the green carpeted tangle of pasture.

Tossing a sliver of light, the moon
cast blossoming shears which fell along my shadowy face.

When the fury of morning creamed yellows appeared,
I wrangled through the shreds of grass and spoke
tenderly to the shroud which swallowed
the flesh of the burrowing moon.

Wooded Echo

Into the hollow echo of the woods,
I look upon the rise of each thread and stitch of fog,
slithering and spread as gauze tangled with warmth.

You loosened the buttons of your blouse as fragrances
toss about the rambling winds and tuck upon each
soothing sting of my flesh and blurring eyes.

In a feverish whimper pouncing between
tree and thicket of thorns,
I reach to touch you and mourn the fading powders
and dissipating flesh.

I lean my ears to the smack of pine to the edge
of the vine coated elm.

Boots scurry through the phantoms of the ancient wood.
I hurry myself as a blossom upon an open wind.

Orchid Bellows to the Rising Myth

Climbing, I find the orchid paused in slumber
high in the reaches of the mountaintop.

A single petal swivels to the rocky path.

Placing this soft and fertile gem in the pouch
of my satchel, I witness the breach of the sky
and I mourn with this slapping rain.

I reach into the myths of the gray thickening sky.

In the dance of each combing cloud,
I hear the lyre pronounce every verb of the gentle earth
which awaits the welcoming muds from the clays
burrowed in the edges of each boulder and deepening root.

As the sun fades to nightfall, swift, the cool moist
rain pats upon the crest of my face and beard.

Clovers at the Depth of Night

As I stood in stillness to the warm
breath of her quivering lips,
sweet clovers pocketing dew and seeped upon our feet.

I grasp the aroma of the painted grooves swelled
deeply in her opened mouth.

Placing my hands upon the curves of her waist,
I feel the tremble of her thighs and motion to the sweat
across each strand of hair which blooms to fullness
by the end of this quivering night.

Milking Acorns

My fingers thumbed through the tome
as leaves scattered across the richness of the Autumn
forest floor, coupling in beds and mounds.

I learned of the ancestor who tosses scents
and spices through the gasping winds.

Stepping across him, I find another, milking the buried acorn
and sunken chestnut.

Leaning the base of my head upon the quivering leaf,
softly, I breath heavy and sulk my lungs with the charms
of this soil which combs along the earth and groaning root.

*After the black quilt of night,*
*I awoke to the thick gray passing clouds*
*and wept with joy.*

Shift as Twilight Comes

The stroking clouds muffled the pulse
and blaze of the noon hour
sun; I wiped the fog and mist from the settling cotton sky as
each fiber crept to the blemish of the earth.

Upon opening my fist to the softness of my palm,
gentle dewdrops gathered and reached my
fingers and thumb with poise.

Leading home the trail spoke of every jagged edge.
I pressed through this gauze which tumbled through the
dance of the deepened fields.

Twilight hummed across the even, slick pasture.
Hurriedly, the sky opened and stung me in the needles
of the stargrown gown of night.

In a blitz, the fog trimmed across the towering mountain
which moaned to the valleys and fields.

I quiver to this slumbering night.

Tender Bones

Moss slept, strode across the forest as felt and velvet garments
Which muttered of the scents blending with
the soft sky, creeping with a sting.

In the pinch of dampness which
harbored upon my cool skin,
I swooned with the tender landscapes and sank so sweetly.

At this moment next year, I revealed my flesh to the grasp
Of slowly wilting leaves and charmed upon the breezes
Which burned beneath the last day of warmth.

The sky moved as a refreshment and
stroked me with a quiet murmur
Of tender bones which spoke to the fragments of Autumn.

## Wicker Chair

I leaned into the cradling arms of the wicker chair.
I pronounced each name of each tree,
grass blade, and chiseled nut.

Slender, the roaming creek fell upon my ankles and feet as
the swelling dance of the opening sky cast trembling shadows
across my face and pale arms.

In moments past the highest arch of the moon,
heat and moisture swabbed along my feverish
flesh.

Swift, the clouds rolling past filled in charcoal grays.
Rain sizzled upon the burn of my moaning flesh.

Shadows blended to shadows cast, I wilted the patterns
of the surmounting velveteen night.

Quietly, I stepped and sank to the smack of blue
sneering light, opened along the heavy sky.

I walked through the edges of the mesh, the sodden fields.

In the exact moment of morning,
tender gushing rays of misty air tangled
me in fevers and pulsing bloods
which rumbled sweetly beneath my feet.

By Nightfall

I rest as the slumber beneath this spade.
Eagerly, I groom myself in the minerals
which reflect each touch
of the soft and tender sky.

Winds slap and tug each spear of grass.

Thousands of rotations across the perfect pause of the sun,
I am filtered to the temperate stream,
from the temperate stream to the bulge of the heaviest ocean,
I belong to you and all your wealth
which mumbles beneath the strokes of the sky.

I perch as a bead of sweat upon the frothy milks
beneath this breast.

Untangling and unweaving, the dance of the particles
on the fastening winds,

I soak to the edge of the moist basting tongue.

By nightfall, I softly walk my way home.

Evening Scene

Crows take to flight upon the lean of treetop to treetop.
Flicked with finger and thumb,
the flat of the stone trembles the film of the pond.

With a 'caw'
the murder lands, rests on the emerald
grass and narrow shoots
which await so patiently.

I kneel to the moss covered log.
My heels dig into the mulch as the warm wind
tosses through my hair.

Beneath the Linen Sheets

Sheets and blankets tossed their way to the hardwood floor,
cascading as silks slid in a gathering of once powdery flesh.

I felt the dance of the moonbeams shatter across the room,
quite alive in all nakedness.

The shout and slithering scream of the once dome of the sky
softened and suckled murmuring
rhythms as my sweat covered
clothing fell across in mounds.

~

From beyond this coast, the smash
Of morning sun relished in the deep of the forest
Which moaned in all sacrament and coveting grip.

I followed the north face of the moss
which coated the damp fumes of each inch of mulch and soil.

Well into the smash of day, I plucked and gathered a few
scents, spices, and aromas.

Next year at this fractured moment, I faced the great
Mountains of the heavy north.

Pale and tired I wept the madness of the tender ocean.

Caught in the Summer Blaze

Following the raindrops as they slanted east,
groomed from a warm host which tossed
spices into the woods which held each bead
as a tightly wound cloth.

Tepid, the ponds which spread and scattered throughout
the heaviness of the moist earth, I
wedged my way from rotted
log to marvels of the greenest kelp.

The heavy spools of the heavy pine, spoke
to me in laughter and slowly undressed before the edge
of Fall.

Now swift in the months of Autumn,
the waltz of the dying rejoice and sweep enigmas
of the glimmering dusts which thresh
across the crimping earth.

By the next morning of Summer, I keep each step, wild
upon the mesh of green and washing warmth
where the mask of the tremouring, shaking pulse
of vein and cups each leaf, I open a gaze of heat
and fall empty upon the soils.

Fields Glazed

Glazed, the glisten of the deep of July
moistens every tread of the weathered wear
of these boots, these ancient denims.

Clovers and lancing spears of grass, I
walk through this field, flooded in emeralds
and the sweet charms of dancing pollens.

Opening with the sting of my eyes, the clouds
filled this tender blue canvas and swarmed
every inch of the dome.

I filled my skin with the flushed press
of the most regal of octaves
of the approaching storms of thick Summer.

Stumble on the Mountainside

The floods suspended in the wealth of the sour gray sky.

Waiting quietly, listened to each slap of the drums
which moaned and tapped the beginning of the sleek
sweat pampering across this edged mountainside.

In a breath, I felt this flesh soak every blast of hot rain.

The fog seduced cliffs and the mountain peak.
I sat upon the sleek crest of the rising climb;
mosses whimpered beneath my feet.

Upon fumbling to the heavy, moist vapors of this realm,
screaming in the madness of the mourning sky,

I felt the grooming particles of edge and trail
as I swept to the glisten of soothing flesh,
my disfigured marrow.

I weep upon this fallen cloak and fading dance of passage.

Phantom in the Late Hour of Autumn

Leaves fell as a phantom sleeping on
the bed of the forest floor.

Gently, the flickering shades of dust
quivered through the loosening
grip of Autumn descent.

I slept, shrouded beneath the ferns,
rising in descent of the weeping
cloak which froze in all mumbling winds.

Softly, I fade to the disenchantment
of this spread, freezing flesh.

I fade through the charms of these ancient woods.

With the clinch of the departed trembling leaves and toss
of the pronouncement of slip and
groan of this pattern of snow,
I walk through the bones, ribs of the earth.

Fist of Leaves

I felt the mint with passing breath
and eager winds draping across my chilled face.

Trembling at the still lurk of the pond,
I wept for the hush of this still, silent place.

Reaching for the slow push of this clever wind,
I smiled upon the flicker of each tossing thread of hair.

As I reached to the tumbling leaves
which spooled across the quiet earth, I
gathered each breast of pages from the oak, elm, and maple.

Into this widow of thrashing night,
I set my feet to the moans of the patient east.

Resting on the Field of Jade

I softened to the tangle of your arms.
Sweet beads, white trembling pearls
fell calmly upon the dredge
of my cuffs and boots.

Smiles upon the lilac as they toss fragrances swift
into the lofting breeze and I stop at each precise moment
and groan with a breath of quiet aroma.

Jades and emeralds of this meadow
slouch as I gingerly walk past.

Listening to the whistles through the treetops, I
call upon the moaning tremors and fastening wrangle
of branch and twig.

I feel my body cease as the blouses and garments of this
threaded heavy navy of night swabs and shrouds my
weakening flesh.

Resurrection

The sun, widespread of the towering oak,
I felt the sauces of this soft Spring rain as each dip
gathered upon the leathery arch of my feet.

An hour later, the dome of surrendering heaven crept
in black clouds and velvet texture which slipped across
each portion of my open flesh.

Seasonings of the rich meadow, so full of bounty,
I gathered the aroma and spoke so gently
of their pinch of fragrance
which led me to the garden where the forest lay.

Resting coddled, I heard the leagues of choirs and orchestras
which bloomed across the most temperate bloom
from these breasts as they fastened into
the soil and wealthy minerals,
I watched calmly and the groan of lusty Spring
crept across me in all weathering grip and poise.

I spoke of the rising covenant in the dwelling clouds
sparse as each threading.

Blackbird Return

I watched the sky breath upon the blackbirds
as song and dance courted across their wings.

With lungs open to the scattered powders of the rigid trail
far past the wet grassy meadow, tossed dashes of peppers
flew well into the chilled, cool horizon
which shouted for the yellows and pinks deeply groomed
across the chiseled east.

I rested upon a smooth, rocky bedstone.
I waited until the next moment of the passing year.
black gems flooded from the apricot sky.

As a tender gift, I gave my brittle bones with dust
and the bloods of my marrow.

Swift, you landed upon me and I gave her the most supple
flesh and rib to mend each softened triumph.

Blouse Loosens

Pages drifted and fumbled, gathered into tomes
from grotto to filtering creek.

Each fiber of each leaf tossed scents of harvest and incense
which settled upon my shirt and jeans.

A few days past and I angered at the frozen grip
of the frozen sky, falling upon me in the whitest veils.

Wind tore the grooming edges of the
snowy glade where I rested;
I watched the blouse loosen to the cupping breath of Winter

as each shred of garment tossed across
this eggshell carpeted floor.

I stopped once more at the icy patches
of the creek which rambled
in a quiet grip of defeat and silence.

Long Shadows of December

On the tan spread of grass by the furthering age of the maple,
I watch as the trembling leaf loosens and takes
flight into the snapping gust of early Winter's wind.

With wrapping arms and this coat which grapples
in wools and thick fibers, soft surrendering
layers of ice and snow
toss distant shards of sunlight, drenched in this sleek
cast of December's shadow.

I rest by the fallen log.

With slight recall, I feel the arms which once held me
in the slippery touch where you sauced each finger across
the edge of my shoulders and nape.

Moments later, I stand upon this bed of white.

I hear you as you whisper across the
field of whistling powders.

Passing Seasons

Beneath the dash of sour rain,
I felt the blemish and threatening touch of the snapping,
crackling branches.

With the passage of drizzling, slouching rivets of the washing
creek, I drank and filled myself, proud this icy drink.

Slowly, I slept in the soils and mulches
from yesterday's Spring.
I feel the tendrils and roots of this aged, proud sycamore.

I offer my flesh to each inch of the pulsing galaxy.

Growing slender, more slender, every pinch of rain and I
soothe the mosses upon the rocks and dancing ferns.

Now, the last slouch of Autumn, I taste
the gust of these fading mints.

Awakening to Stillness

Through this flesh,
I felt the thud, course of her bloods.

I roamed the endless meadows of her abdomen and waist.

As my neck rested upon her warm face and cheeks,
I heard the floods from the slapping rains
which threaded across the swollen river, still
stained in greens and dark grays of the rigid rocks.

I awoke to stillness.
every passing hour suckled my denim cuffs and leather boots.

With slippery thick breasts,
I quietly watched the fertile hills as they groomed each
pasture and coiling river.

Lavender Blouse

She opened her lavender blouse and loosened as soft
rain pattering through the wind, landing on edge and inch.

Reaching for her, I traveled through her as vapors
glanced across me, slow the falling clouds.

I found myself upon the woodland trail;
slowly, the riveting trickle of fresh water scoured across me.

Spotting the elm tree, I stopped and rested until
every grooming ledge of the dripping cloth
swept past both legs and pronouncement of the torso
in which I held sultry breath.

Once more, I reached for the fullness
of her breads and warmth
flooding past with the hot gusts of Summer winds.

Carving Fingers

I traveled to the jagged, peak of the mountainside.

Sparsely covered pine trees carried their lonely breath;
sweats of the soft rain drizzled in fumbling hot clay and dirt.

Gently, I carved my fingers through the
fullness of her almond colored hair.

She spoke of thirst and the frequent
gushing touch of latitude.

Upon reaching the dip of the valley and
all it's fields and meadows,
scores of the flight of the purple finch
threaded across the descension of this scattered trail.

With moistening soil, I felt the depresses of my sore feet
as the pebbles and rocks edged into my boot.

With a warm wind, she blushed across
me in arrows and chipped
snap of the pinecone which fell in
covenant to the heavy earth.

*I search for an endless travelway surrounding the earth.*

*Sweetly, I fade in a crisp wind.*

*Fallen dust, I warm beneath the heavy sun.*

Puzzles

The sky clouds broke and thinned in puzzles.

Winding river, each slap of gushing
water spread as tender lips
blushing across the channel and coves.

I pressed the palm of this hand and guided my way through
the softness of your waist and the dampness of your
sweet trembling thighs.

Clovers swept, roamed across the nearby field.
I dredged these heavy feet and gathered
each lavish bead of water.

From the wash of the sky,
saplings quivered and danced through the winds and
shook to the closeness of the current.

After the madness of the seemingly ceaseless storm,
I walked into the bog so near the flooded edge.

Each hour froze and tumbled through this shivering crisp
day of the earliest Spring.

Loss

Gnarled and coated with knots, lengthy and stretched, each
nook of this ancient branch spoke with the cry of the wind.

Standing before these verbs of a heavy groan, I softly
traced my finger and thumb in these
seductions of the Summer woods.

Surpassing this artifact, warm cascading
winds from the blooming
lungs, draped across with gentle breath, I further myself

with every step.

In the deepest breeze of the majesty of midnight,
I still hear each creak of the proud gasping
wood, lumber and branch.

My ears weaken with every moan.
well into the next particle of day,
I listen to the snap and softly I unburdone myself.

Waiting With the Willow Tree

I stood so near this weeping willow tree.
Thick, the green glades softened my feet.

With this glaze, furthest in the arms of Autumn, I
feel the coolest rains tap upon the crest of my shoulders.

Alongside the keenest glance to the snap of the elm leaf,
this sleeve of parchment takes, loosens to the blush of the sky.

I wait until evening when the powders of the threads
of these leaves fragment in softness.

I wait for the slumbering snows of a yearning December.

Particles of Preservation

Alive with the snapping winds, the earth
hardened and fumbling ancient leaves screamed
across the dead bones of the wintery landscape.

Swallows of the hottest coffee stung and scraped
through my throat.

Humid pillowing of a steamy breath, I
edged my way through the garden glen,
masked in icy patches and frost covered grass.

I moaned until morning as the floundering sky
opened before me and each particle of preservation
drew my bloods in thick sauces and silently,
I felt the sting of this Winter undress me in cloth.

Awoken I Cast the Longest Shadow

Endless pillows and sharp edges of cascading linens,
I soak each fragrant aroma into the well of my lungs.

Warmth basting through the room falls upon
every stitch of my woolen shirt and tenderly trembling sweat
flickers on the crest of my forehead as I navigate
in this broken compass of a room.

Further along in the fractured grimace of morning, I
search the garden as a platform and hunt the jousting
most northern star.

I cast this shadow deep into the robe of the glen.

In the Attic Room

I dredged my lips across the smooth
slope of her straining muscles.

At the precise fracture of morning,
softly my temples and cheeks
rested with glinting dusts which danced across the attic room.

Soaked, I drip upon this wellspring of youth
as the spinning pause of the sun welcomes me in rhythms.

~

I walk the path through the wood.
Cool, tender breezes moan and mumble along the heated
pastes of my shoulders and back as I snap the limbs
depressed beneath my foot.

I find you in the garden and smell you in the glen
as your heavy breasts breath a discord of hushing waves
across each edge of my flesh.

~

I recall the sweet fibers of your full bloomed hair.

Leaves Hung of the Frozen Floor

Soaked, the leaves slipped through the river rapids
and threaded upon the fallen branch and jagged rocks.

With perfect pronunciation, the maples outstretched
and undressed upon every sweep of cool, chilled water.

Fading into the shroud of gray lowering clouds,
every crisp scent of the cooled surrounding forest

Threw the muscled frozen earth and cast these patient aromas
freshly into the spooling dance of spreading waters.

I stood wrapped in early winter winds as mulch
and embedded pebbles spoke of quiet
dancing and quivering cloaks.

I quest my way through the winds of a moaning drench
where the riverbank swelled.

Thrashing naked, the yellow and heavy tan leaves
hung as a quilt upon the frost on the edge of the forest floor.

Spread of Apricot

Into the floods of daylight,
softly, I watch each bleeding slick spread of apricot
as tense slender clouds hug the coast in triumph.

Scarce, the pine grove, well into the growth,
I stamp upon the chipped, nutted pinecones
and return my sight to these damp hues and bloods.

Across the dome, flickering in blues, I
cascade my gaze and watch the heaviest grays beyond.
Each sponges their way in drizzling rain, so distant

The fractured crest sweeps in trembling fog.

I pause by the softest soil.
with a fistful of mist, my boots tamp
as every patch of meadow warms slowly beneath me.

Earliest Moment

I stepped my way into the wood.
Quickly, I began listening to the press of my feet
with snap and crunch of the fallen
twigs, leaves and rotted logs.

I sulked my way through the fog and
webbed quilt upon the treetops.

Winds fell as a drizzle through every
wooded arms and thick trunk.

Gingerly, my eyes stung their way
through the approach of the meadow.

I broomed my way across spears of grassy patches.

My senses stung upon the onion sprouts
as I lanced through the threshold and
quivered to the patience
of the earliest moment of Spring.

Golds

As I looked upon her in the bed of down,
lulls of passing, glittering dust fell across the room.

Deep in the passage through the heavy darkness
of the latest afternoon,

I rose to the fullness and posture of the cool, trembling chill
which coiled and wedged upon the slow movement of her
feet and tension of her calves.

I carved through the sheets and groomed my way
as the tremble of her glistening thighs bloomed as a meadow,
silent and sleek.

Motioning my way, I walked the golds of her coast.

Ribs of Autumn

With the tap and press of my leather wrapped feet, I
stepped upon the softest earth and roamed my way
upon the softest rib, bent deeply into the soil which
scoured tenderly this rooted oak.

Countless, the bones reaching into its marrow;
heavily the altar of the ground grew
fattened by the Autumn dash of leaves.

I leaned and scathed against the shredding bark.
Quietly, the acorns reached farthest
into the pinch of fading leaves, gathering dust.

I slept through the deep of Winter.
I awoke to the glistening webs of the sprouting grass.

Soothingly, I approach the rise of the warming sun.

Searching for the Coast

The creek emptied freshly into the gash of the river;
softly the slicing words of kelp and jettison rocks
Dredged in ancient rhythms.

As I rest upon the frigid, spouting driftwood,
I slouch in breathing fog which wraps and grips
the heavy green water, passing in rising floods.

Upon the return of the warm, thick wind,
I thumb my way through the madness of this spreading moss.

I betray the northern wind and travel
east as the sun endlessly dances upon me.

I search for the tanned and leathery, rock filled coast.
The horizon fell in trim and well groomed slivers
where the snapping edge faded into silence.

Opened as Goblets

I wade in the gloating width of the river,
soft in greens and edging foams upon the shore.

Washed upon the waist, my abdomen quivered
and shook to the blanching winds of the deepest
moment in Autumn.

~

Dressing on the shoreline, I knelt and
touched the trembling water
as I felt the cupping palm of her hand

grace tenderly alongside my thigh and screaming groin.

~

I left well into the narrow slice of woods
which carpet me in moss and crumbling leaves.

As I open my mouth, moaning with
the cup of the empty goblet,
I drank and absorbed the fragrance of each
curving dance and soft aroma.

Seeds Upon the Wind

I groomed through the pastures of wheat.

Tenderly, the breathing winds soothed across my face,
both angle and whipping lash of the fullness of my
hair, soft colored brown.

Floods and flurries of seeded dust,
I sank my feet into the soil and rocky dirt.

In the precision of this sweeping moment where
gales slapped against me,

I stepped to the creek.

I drank in madness as a child to a full, milky, warm breast.

Slender, waving gusts of particles dancing upon the wind,
heavy arms trembled upon the flesh of my torso.

Each stalk of wheat spoke to me of the dew beads
and the christening of early Autumn.

Return to the Fields in the Mourning Hour

The dome of the sky robed across the thin edges in velvets.

Ripe, the orchard pressed thick roots into the soil
as I rest upon the trunk, moaning to these ancient bones.

Vast, the spread of the canvas of empty night, I needled my
eyes and shook a silent grasp upon these
crimping hands and crimping feet.

~

I look at the trellise of your almond colored hair,
dampened by hour in this field of chipped stalks,
burrowed pebbles and scattered oaks.

Well into the tremble of soaked morning,
I walked swift into the gathered roaming fields
which filled my empty lungs with clover and patches of mint.

~

Rains pelted every pasted inch of my cooled flesh.
Into the tempered crisp beads,
I look upon this and watch you unfold.

Waiting

I raced my fingers along the chipped and weathered fence.

Looking upon the distant, proud
haunch of the mountaintop,
the rains carved through to the valley
where I stood, awaiting the soothing, cool wash.

The naked hook of my toes
opened softly, groaning the words and humming the vowels
of salvation as this soil began to moisten.

My cloth and fabric of my clothes sulked behind me.
I walked through these emerald and jade
with each step as I tenderly vanished and faded

into the endlessness of the trembling grassy fields.

Back to the Forest

The air grew warmer as
I stepped closer to the exit of the forest..

Hearing the snapping beak and throat of the mourning dove,
I watched her gather seeds and bury
each feathered wing beneath the slicing breeze.

I sat nearest the maple tree and slept for the sliver of time
when I can deepen through the cooler and distant patch
of forest where the doves would gather by nightfall.

By the Cove

Stopping with you along the way,
hair flickered across temples and ears;
I pressed the edge of my lips upon the dashing sweats
coating from neck to breasts.

Here sitting by the cove,
the water coated and buried against the kelp covered
rocks which rose as a dome.

I looked back to her and she had vanished with the pink,
purple and gray splash of the evening sky.

Coated in Gold

She shook through the cold December,
rattling as a sapling pine, buried roots soon to coat in ices.

I asked her for the nakedness of her hands,
I placed them upon the warmth of my abdomen
and the hot burn of my face and neck.

Her flesh, colored in the skins of the olive;
I pressed my ears upon her breads and satchels of milk,
the wrapping wind stole across the ocean bay.

With the thought of my conception,
we danced sweetly along the sands, coated in gold.

With the thought of your conception,
we danced sweetly along the sands, coated in gold.

Fade of Her Shadow

With swollen breads, I listened to the fabric of the room,
dust of the pillow and gown quivers
of lips which speaks of full
pouches of creams; here I purr in rhythms and softened
to the concave press of the soaked and
trembling threads of the bed.

Peering with a sting and roam of my gaze,
I followed the earliest flurries which dampened the earth
only to submit to the approaching breeze;
I hear the song of the patterned white fleece

groaning in the fields which surround.

She walks across the tender lace as the breath echoed.
Fogs lifted to the most distant pierce of the mountaintop,
I watched her as the icy tremble of
the sky opened the flanking
gate of the west and night pronounced itself and softened

me with black pillows which slouched
from the tender heaven.

Quietly, I watched her leave and exhaust herself
with frost and the bite of each trembling
sneer of Winter's chill.

Bluebird

Perched on the twig, wrestling in the cool breath of Autumn,
the bluebird sang with a full, heavy colored breast.

I look to her neck and clavicle,
sweetly, she tosses a palm and traces minuettes along the edge
of my quivering lips.

Again, I reach to her.
All that remains of her
blooms in throated chirps upon the chilled wind
which carries sweet leaves into the foggy current;
vanished into the mist and calm rains.

Ocean Walk in the Deep of Night

The oils washed from a thousand voices, once held
in the deep.

Groomed into the saps and rains from
the deepest hues of gray,
I slipped the cup of my palm, so
tenderly upon her, I smelled the
cascading water from the spread
of the madness of the ocean.

She eagerly quivered as a jellyfish, soaked
upon the golden crest and curve of the shoreline.

Gently, I turned to her and found the choirs of ancient birds
and endless slap of the salted brine sweep across
the sands and polish every dune as shouted by the last flight
of the seagull, roaming the sweet rippling gush of a distant
water.

Into the salve of a moist and suckling sulk where
salts speak in hymnals and psalms,

The sky opened before my stung and flooded eyes.
Silently, I wavered through the thicket
of kelp, stones, and shells.

I heard her gasp upon the burning leathers of my face.

Blood Upon the Grass of Jade

With delivery, I slumbered in these bloods, mulch,
rich and soaked soils as I walk this
forest in leaves which fumble, the
sound of crackling branches.

To the glaze of the maple tree, I humble and offer
each drizzle to the passing cloth and forgotten pause of the
slight dash, the scurry of birds.

I feel the thorns as they wrap across the flesh of this bark.

With sweet scents and passing lusty
chymes of the mint leaves
which find passage, I empty my bloods upon the jade grasses
and soon I am lost in this wood.

White Petal

Now Spring, the mountains fog lifts, then dissipates
only to fall as mist.

I stand as the cherry blossom, catching dew upon the petals
and reflecting white shine across the garden.

Watching you come to me as the bamboo shoots,
the threads of the meadow's grass.

I taste the sweet nectar of your tears
as you rest beneath me in flushed skins
of the starlit sky, shining.

I look upon you in the fertile growth,
swelling milks of your aching breasts.

In an instant, a white petal falls, then rests upon
your shoulder, only to take swiftly to the wind.

Remembrances by the Garden

From the flesh of the apricot, I extracted all nectar
and flurried juices into the deep of my throat.

Softly, I felt the press of your breasts against
my back. The fat warmth of the Spring sun

tosses light and fractures shadows into the length
of the garden's grotto, bundled as a satchel,
fallen beneath the tease of the rain.

She hid perfectly in the soils of the soft earth.
Gingerly, her tastes and juices linger in my mouth.

*In the last moment of Autumn,*

*I gather the crimping leaf.*

Passages

I threaded my fingers through the fullness and silks
of your walnut hair, tossed upon the breathing wind,
tossed in waves from the cool breadth of the heaven's dome.

Your lips stretched as the floods of the river
which spoke of the fog, now lifted to the treetops.

Feeling the soil deepen beneath me, I
spoke of enchantment where the mint leaves grow
and flickers upon the dancing breath of rippling waters.

Your full, soft breasts trembled as a passage,
a rich meadow with milks reserved in the shoots,
the barley which held every angle and gathered beads
of moisture.

Quietly, I place the seed in the thick palm of my hand.
I hear her speak of distant realms where each
touch fattens and slithers into the earth.

Hollow of the Pocket

I stretch my arms across her in perfect composition.

As the clever whimper tugged through the edge of her lips
and breath so warm across me, I felt
the cool sweat of her neck
meld to the bow and curve of my hands.

Wrestling across this fracture,
I moan as each particle takes to the soothing rivets
of the wind.

Your fragrance and spice wallows across every grooming
touch where we lay in the field, coddled by the bloom
and so near, we lurk to the broadness of the oak.

I take a sliver of the trunk of the wood
and place it in the hollow of this deep pocket.

By early Autumn, dusts loosen across the room where we lay.

Entering the Passage of Winter

Leaves coated in the dredge of the blanket of Fall,
I stood in the toss of billowing dust.

Standing on the ledge overlooking the soft
passage of the deep of the trembling stream,

I breath the crisp sweep of a tumbling wind
which enters the quaking, yearning
desires of these open lungs.

I feel the bloods coursing through my veins.
I feel the water suckling at my feet and fondling

in silence before me as a flourish of the soon arrival
of blooming Winter.

Into the tempest of this scream of the groin
which fondles as a spread, the dusts of snow,

I stand and revere the quiet hush of this grooming sky.

Dipped in the Wilt of Autumn

The pond opened as a trembling mouth,
alive in fog and hanging mist.

Alive from the watery deep, I looked upon her
as she slipped out of the kelp driven water.

Softly, the fullness of her heavy brown hair
roamed and swept along her back and slender

shoulders. I spoke to her of the masks
which arrive in Autumn
and paste the wilt of the forest floor.

Upon the Mountaintop

The wind fell upon me,
cascading endless words of the distant mountain
and regal glow.

Verbs rubbed from my lips and tongue;
sweet snows hung from trail to cascading cliff.

I heard the mumbling evergreen,
tender moisture soaked as velvets against the passing breeze.

I paused at the clifftop.
gingerly, my feet deepened through the fullness
where snows richened against my leather boot.

Now, standing into the laughing air,
rich in the decisive sting where the open
breath slapped against my tender face,

I soaked in the broadness of the reach of the jagged peak.

Quilt

I edge my sight through the night sky.
Swift, the sting of the needled points, the diamonds
shake through the grove of my flesh.

I soften upon this grass filled field.
Waves of the onion sprout hushes to
me in the most tender speech
as the mushroom patches answer me in their starving root.

I blush as the moon bears it's breast,
so full and soft;
slowly, gingerly, the fullness of the spreading cloud
crawls into the open flesh of velvet night.

The cool winds of this early Autumn night,
I open so cleverly as I carve my way
upon her and fill myself in the laughter of tender shadows
which sulk and croon into my clever face;
I spool the threads of her linens and open
her as a quilt on the bed of this grooming earth.

Winter Shoal

I soak my flesh in the chilled Winter's breath
as each fiber of my coat and wools
ice against the fever of my crisp layered skin,
quiet and alive.

The heaven shook and quaked in floods.

I felt the jagged earth moan beneath my trembling feet
with the stones and patches of ice prowl
to the suckling grip of sweet sleekness,
the most tender dying earth.

I stand alone on the iced grasses of the meadow.
Winds prowl across my face and the raw flesh of my neck.
I wear this cloak, this Winter shoal.

Rains in the Bay

Chilled, the water of the curving bay
spread along the rocks and gathered sands of the edge
where silks soaked and salts dredged.

Cloaked and gushing clouds opened before
the threads of this gloated water,
flourishing from the gash of the sky.

Each tremble of tapping rains
gathered and spirited the fattening bay.

I press my lips to this hot, steamy cup of coffee
and stood so soaked as I stood before this
full, flooding sauce of groaning drench.

Rain Storm

Upon the first moment of Spring,
the earth, tender felt, suckled the sole of my foot.

I dredged my way from tender growth
which ushered forth the grains of the nearest field
and clipped the dampness of every passage
of drizzling rains, tapping upon my shoulder, neck and
moistening hair.

Reaching the fields of maize,
I swept passed the stiff, eager stalks
and broomed passed the cake of the earth.

I heightened my way to the hilltop.
I slept in the soaking, cool rain as each
withered inch of my flesh
coiled beneath the most sopping thread and fiber of clothing.

Thin Stem

I spoke to the trembling breeze
which coated Winter ices upon the dampness
of my flesh.

At the thin stem where Autumn ends,
I plucked the last gathering of grasses,
slippery in their eager frost and fading bounty.

The field flooded in the tan and reddest leaves
as my feet swept and glanced through them,
tenderly alive.

Moaning across me, the sky
plucked every crisp shred of my face
and chilled the cool threads of my chestnut hair.

Well into the approach of Winters breath,
I sauced and shook with the dancing wind.

Chipped and Wooden

Branch, twig, and stem thinned in the gush,
broom of Autumn's breeze.

I suspended the quivering laughter from
the blushing empty arms,
the leaves quivered to the haunches of
the earth, sleek and frozen.

I gathered the fallen acorn in the chilled
palm of my hand.

Well into the shreds of the shaking nakedness
of the full body of Spring, I opened the earth.

Gingerly, I planted the nut, chipped and wooden as
the flesh of this parcel of life swabbed in the tremble
of the combing soil.

## By the Pond

Alive in the breath of nightfall,
Sweet flavors of the patches of mint and the trembling
Spot of clover, I stepped fluidly through each,
Moisture poised upon my ankle and foot.

Stopping and near the greenest lurk
Of kelp, the rippling edges of the water
Cascaded across her hair and full breasts.

I opened my senses to the drafts of a quiet aroma.
She stepped so near me.
I fell upon the soft paints of her swooning lips.

Vest and Fiber

The sun flickered a soft warmth across the valley's spread
roaming in the deep of the mountain's descent.

I rest upon the coaxing splash of moss,
alive in the most tender hue of green.

Each toss of the fondling leaves
scattered through the temptation of Autumn's approaching
vest and fiber.

I spoke into the splashing tremble of the cooling winds.

Mercy

Into the sounds of the weeping woods,
the softest moss, whisper of the ferns and hush
of the cluttered leaves,
I feel the press of my feet upon the welcome
of the soils thrown like carpets.

Knelt by the bush tamping the course of the full bloomed
river, I wash my face, hands and look to the sky;
gray swivels across in fattened rain, clouds.

I follow the thinning trail.
I deepen into the gloating mercy of the heavy woods.

Chasing the Endless Court

The roots starved for a pouch, pocket of mud
which held, fell upon a tangle of moisture;
alive, the heavy earth bloomed in quiet promise.

I touched the glaze of the spread, glistening moss.
tenderly, the fading sun dipped across the horizon
and I soaked into the velveteen nights sky.

Full, the breast, open and pale
fastened upon me as the fleshy doughs
arrived with the nimble nooks of my back and shoulders.

As the morning sun rose smartly in the east,
I fled and chased the endless court of
a deepened curving night.

Creek

Sliding fingers and thumbs,
I gathered each trembling white bead of sweat
and spoke to her of the grotto and the
slice of the moan of the creek.

I placed my lips upon the endless, perfect stretch
where her clavicle burrowed deep.

~

Her groaning throat opened and spoke
as the draft of the empty castle, both room
and cool stone corridor.

~

I traveled this earth laden grotto,
gently upon the trail while spooling gasps of wind
loosened the tuck of her hair.

As partnership, I gripped the aromas of her pausing flesh.
Soft patter of the falling, swollen rains,
I step upon the tender soils and rest
by the sauces of the channel
and watch the driftwood coil at the slight rapids,
sulking in a tumble and swoon.

Garment and Jacket

The grass slouched as woven yarn
as the wools of the willow tree spoke of the wild
earth and the lust of the countryside.

I felt the sting of the frosty lake
as small icy waves spun across me in search
of the smoothest flavors, peach and the groin of the soil.

Endless, the carved white ruin of the dead
stretch of the forest,
I touched the dead root, mulch of the Autumn leaf.

Gray pasture of the flooded open sky,
I spoke of thirst and the sky sliced a gash.

Most quietly, the snows and spindling breeze
tremored and danced upon the swollen fibers of my
garment and jacket.

Fleece

Loosely, the branches slung, spoke
of the wooden verbs which
rattle with each smash of coming Winter.

I leaned upon the vexed, gnarled bark
which soothed each pinch of flesh and
tang of the buried bone.

Softly, I sang to the roots as each fiber
rose to a peak, then calmed in a deepened and mapped clay
so swelled beneath the stretching floor, blankets
where snowbeds trembled.

I left this place where the bones of each ancestor slept.
The rib curved across the sweet tangle of the earth
as I guided my foot upon packs of fleece
and the frost of snowy fields.

In the Garden

The garden stretched to the full bloom of the sun,
quivered beneath the breasted girth of the moon;
I swivelled and swam beneath the silks of the garment
she wore, soft and alive.

Threading and gingerly, I spoke to the pulsing
waters which swelled along the patches of spices
and the creeping moan of each tender soil.

I stopped, engulfed the probing dance of the heavy sky.

Well into the fullness of my wild hair,
quietly, the rain tapped upon my face;
I crimped and wilted as the cherry blossom

faded with the course of the smash of Autumn's grip.

Egret

I strangled the serpent which rested in the open
mouth of the open fattening slosh of the heaviest ocean.

The overhang of the trees trembled across each throb
where the cove splashed and slithered.

Buoys stabbed the whitest caps and reared across
every slippery fangs as swift dashes of wind

cascaded across the fresh crimping boat and fisherman
sipping the blackest coffee on the soft sands of the shore.

~

The egret darted across the waves and patterns of the tuck,
nip of a hush where the mad temper of the salted
water thickened lavish upon the roam of the deep.

As He Waits for Spring

These curtains cloak the moonlight which drips
across the smoothest window.

I listen to the tapping rain,
I listen to the hushing dance of the wind, alive
in all it's girth;
I can smell the fragrance of the distant mountain,
all the lakes scattered with the raw slapping waters.

The grasses prune the brown patches of dead earth
as spears and blades return to the shades of lusty green.

I cup into the deep of the down bed.
Flickered dusts rest upon the pillow and thick
stretch of the burlap blanket;

I walk the room in madness.
I wait for the soaked sweet flavors of the field
to open in silence; I pause and turn back into the folds
of the fresh angle of morning dew.

*I close my eyes...wait.*

# *About the Author*

**Donny Barilla**, a poet covering the realms: human intimacy, nature, mythology, theology, and man's relationship with death and the departed, has been writing for over three decades. He writes daily and strives to renew himself as an artist from page to page and body of work to body of work. Very seldom does he take a break from writing as he views it as a full-time job. He lives a reclusive lifestyle and finds himself clinging close to nature and all her elements. His home state of Pennsylvania strikes chords of poetic depth about him as he finds loveliness from cornfield to meadow. Whether it's feelings of love, intimacy, or a special closeness, he maintains the feeling that death does not take these with him/her to the grave. Emotions and feeling outlast the flesh of the human body. Human intimacy draws near an enigmatic spiritual passion which conquers all on the prismatic scale of experience. When speaking of mythology Donny says, "myths were created to make sense of feelings which are complicated by very nature. They are perhaps more easily understood through persons greater than oneself. As for theology, a disciplined aspect, incorporates quite finely with passions and secured poetic comforts.

https://twitter.com/BarillaDonny

www.ingramcontent.com/pod-product-compliance
Lightning Source LLC
Chambersburg PA
CBHW032229080426
42735CB00008B/776